The Award Winning Songs
of the
COUNTRY MUSIC ASSOCIATION

UPDATED 2ND EDITION (1984-1991)

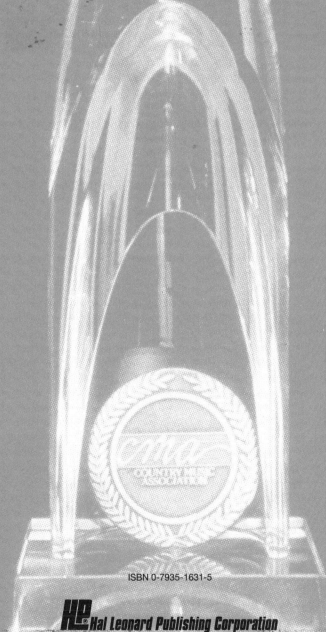

ISBN 0-7935-1631-5

HL**®**Hal Leonard Publishing Corporation
7777 West Bluemound Road P.O. Box 13819 Milwaukee, WI 53213

The
Award Winning Songs
of the
COUNTRY MUSIC ASSOCIATION

Through the Country Music Association's leadership and guidance, Country Music has become one of America's most diplomatic ambassadors to the world. Industry leaders readily admit that CMA has won global recognition and has been the most important force in the worldwide growth and expansion of Country Music. The first trade organization ever formed to promote a type of music, CMA, founded in 1958, originally consisted of only 233 members and now boasts more than 7,600 members in 31 countries.

One of CMA's most significant achievements is its annual awards show which has been on national television since 1968. Considered the Country Music industry's most highly-coveted and pre-eminent awards, the accolades are presented annually to outstanding Country artists and songwriters, as voted by CMA's membership, to honor excellence in artistry. Membership in CMA is open to those persons or organizations presently or formerly active, directly or substantially, in the field of Country Music.

The second edition of *The Award Winning Songs of the Country Music Association* features the official top five songs nominated for CMA Song of the Year from 1984 to 1991. Any Country Music song with original words and music is eligible based upon the song's Country singles chart activity during the eligibility period, which spans from July 1 through June 30 of each year. Nominations from the CMA membership, in addition to the top five songs from the combined tabulation of the Country singles charts from *Billboard*, *Cashbox*, *The Gavin Report*, and *Radio & Records*, are voted on through balloting by the entire CMA membership. From this, the top five songs appear on the final ballot with Song of the Year being selected and first announced on the CMA Awards telecast. The entire balloting process is conducted by the international accounting firm of Deloitte Touche.

The award for Song of the Year goes to the songwriter or songwriters.

We hope you will enjoy all of the selections.

ONTENTS

Award Winning Songs Of The CMA
Updated 2nd Edition (1984-1991)

Also Available:
THE AWARD WINNING SONGS OF THE COUNTRY MUSIC ASSOCIATION
FIRST EDITION
Featuring all of the official top five songs nominated for CMA Song Of The Year
from 1967 to 1983. Includes 80 selections. (00359485)

MA Song Of The Year

CMA AWARD-WINNING SONGWRITERS

Photo Courtesy of CMA/
Don Putnam, Photographer

JEFF SILBAR and LARRY HENLEY
1984 – "Wind Beneath My Wings"

Photo Courtesy of CMA/
Don Putnam, Photographer

LEE GREENWOOD
1985 — "God Bless The U.S.A."

Photo Courtesy of CMA/
Beth Gwinn, Photographer

DON SCHLITZ, RANDY TRAVIS (Performer) and PAUL OVERSTREET
1986 — "On The Other Hand"

Photo Courtesy of CMA/
Alan Mayor, Photographer

DON SCHLITZ, PAUL OVERSTREET and RANDY TRAVIS (Performer)
1987 — "Forever And Ever, Amen"

Photo Courtesy of CMA/
Beth Gwinn, Photographer

K.T. OSLIN
1988 — "80's Ladies"

Photo Courtesy of CMA/
Beth Gwinn, Photographer

MAX D. BARNES (with VERN GOSDIN)
1989 — "Chiseled In Stone"

*Photo Courtesy of CMA/
Beth Gwinn, Photographer*

JON VEZNER and DON HENRY
1990 — "Where've You Been"

*Photo Courtesy of CMA/
Alan L. Mayor, Photographer*

VINCE GILL AND TIM DUBOIS
1991 — "When I Call Your Name"

NOMINATED SONG OF THE YEAR
WRITERS AND/OR PERFORMERS

Photo Courtesy of CMA/
Alan Mayor, Photographer

GEORGE STRAIT

Photo Courtesy of CMA/
Beth Gwinn, Photographer

RANDY TRAVIS

Photo Courtesy of CMA/
Beth Gwinn, Photographer

NAOMI and WYNONNA/THE JUDDS

Photo Courtesy of CMA/
Alan Mayor, Photographer

DAN SEALS

Photo Courtesy of CMA/
Alan Mayor, Photographer

HOLLY DUNN

Photo Courtesy of CMA
Beth Gwinn, Photographer

JAMIE O'HARA and KIERAN KANE/THE O'KANES

CMA AWARDS SHOW PHOTOS

DAVE LOGGINS and ANNE MURRAY

*Photo Courtesy of CMA/
Beth Gwinn, Photographer*

RONNIE MILSAP and KENNY ROGERS

*Photo Courtesy of CMA/
Alan Mayor, Photographer*

WILLIE NELSON and KRIS KRISTOFFERSON

Photo Courtesy of CMA/
Beth Gwinn, Photographer

HANK WILLIAMS, JR.

Photo Courtesy of CMA
Don Putnam, Photographer

WILLIE NELSON and KRIS KRISTOFFERSON

Photo Courtesy of CMA/
Beth Gwinn, Photographer

REBA McENTIRE

Photo Courtesy of CMA
Don Putnam, Photographer

JEFF COOK, TEDDY GENTRY, MARK HERNDON and RANDY OWEN – ALABAMA

Photo Courtesy of CMA/
Alan Mayor, Photographer

LORETTA LYNN and CONWAY TWITTY

Photo Courtesy of CMA
Don Putnam, Photographer

WILLIE NELSON, KRIS KRISTOFFERSON, WAYLON JENNINGS and JOHNNY CASH

Photo Courtesy of CMA/
Beth Gwinn, Photographer

TANYA TUCKER

Photo Courtesy of CMA/
Beth Gwinn, Photographer

DWIGHT YOAKAM and BUCK OWENS

Photo Courtesy of CMA/
Beth Gwinn, Photographer

KATHY MATTEA

Photo Courtesy of CMA/
Beth Gwinn, Photographer

HANK WILLIAMS , JR.

Photo Courtesy of CMA/
Beth Gwinn, Photographer

REBA McENTIRE

Photo Courtesy of CMA/
Beth Gwinn, Photographer

GARTH BROOKS

Photo Courtesy of CMA/
Beth Gwinn, Photographer

DON HENRY, KATHY MATTEA, and JON VEZNER

Photo Courtesy of CMA/
Alan L. Mayor, Photographer

PAM TILLIS

Photo Courtesy of CMA/
Alan L. Mayor, Photographer

VINCE GILL and PATTY LOVELESS

Photo Courtesy of CMA/
Alan L. Mayor, Photographer

CLINT BLACK and ROY ROGERS

AFTER ALL THIS TIME

Words and Music by
RODNEY CROWELL

ALL MY EX'S LIVE IN TEXAS

Country shuffle (♩♩ played as ⌐³┐♩♪)

Words and Music by SANGER D. SHAFER
and LINDA J. SHAFER

All my ex-'s live in Tex-as, and Tex-as is a place__ I'd dear-ly

CODA

E   A

fore   I   re - side___ in Ten - nes - see.

D   D#   E   D   D#

Some folks think I'm   hid - ing.

E   D   D#   E

It's   been ru - mored that I   died.   But I'm a - live and well___

A   D6 D#dim7 A/E   A6/9

___ in Ten - nes - see.

BABY'S GOT HER BLUE JEANS ON

Words and Music by BOB McDILL

Moderately Fast

Down on the cor-ner by the traf-fic light ev'-ry-bod-y's look-in'

as she goes by.___ They turn their heads___ and they watch her till___ she's gone.___

Lord, have mer-cy! Ba - by's got her blue jeans on.___

A BETTER MAN

Words and Music by CLINT BLACK
and HAYDEN NICHOLAS

Moderately fast

What do you say when it's o - ver? _____ Don't know

if I should say an - y - thing at all. _____

Yes I'm

Yes I'm

leav - in' here a bet - ter man.

BOP

Words and Music by PAUL DAVIS
and JENNIFER KIMBALL

CHISELED IN STONE

Words and Music by VERN GOSDIN
and MAX D. BARNES

Moderately slow

You ran cry-in' to the bed-room; I ran off to the bar;

See addtional lyrics

an-oth-er piece of heav-en gone to hell. The

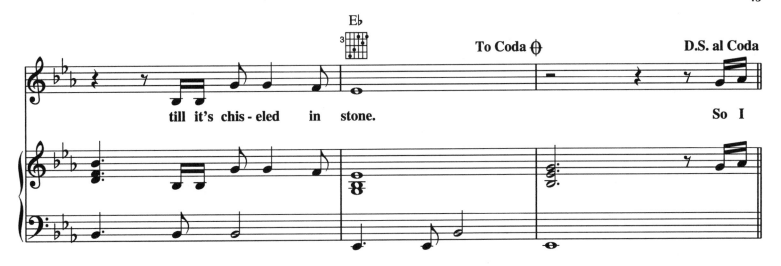

Additional Lyrics

2. Then an old man sat beside me
   And looked me in the eye.
   He said, "Son, I know what you're goin' through.
   But you oughta get down on your knees
   And thank your lucky stars
   That you've got someone to go home to."
   Chorus

3. So I brought these pretty flowers
   Hopin' you would understand
   Sometimes a man is such a fool.
   These golden words of wisdom
   From the heart of that old man
   Showed me I ain't nothin' without you.
   Chorus

CAN'T STOP MY HEART FROM LOVIN' YOU

Words and Music by JAMIE O'HARA
and KIERAN KANE

Moderately bright (♪♪ played as ♪³♪)

Late - ly your love_____
self_____

is a cold, cold rain_____
I'm a gon - na go._____

com - in' down on
I pull out on my

DADDY'S HANDS

Words and Music by
HOLLY DUNN

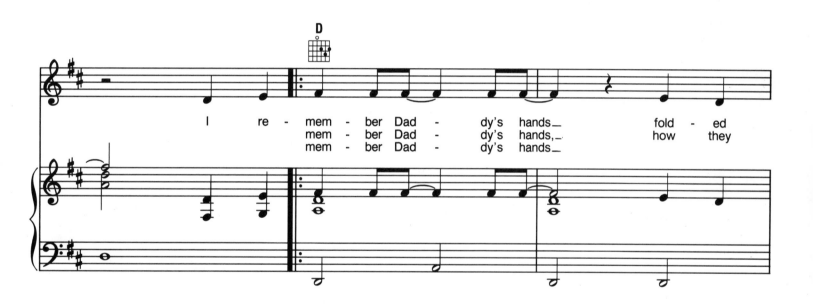

I re- mem- ber Dad- dy's hands_ fold- ed
mem- ber Dad- dy's hands,_ how they
mem- ber Dad- dy's hands_

si- lent- ly in prayer,_ and reach- ing out to hold_
held my Ma- ma tight_ and pat- ted my_ back
work- ing 'til they bled,_ sac- ri- ficed un- self-

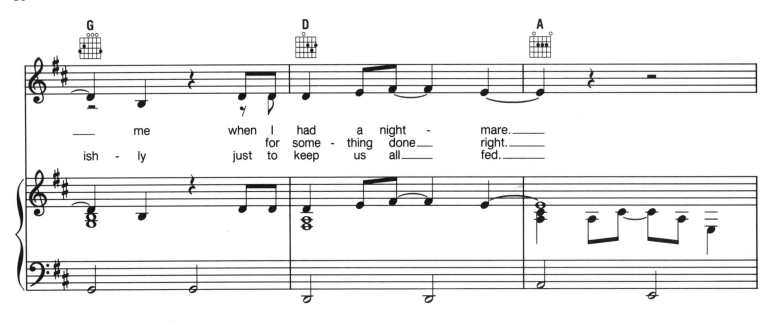

me when I had a night - mare.___
ish - ly just to keep us all___ fed.___
for some - thing done___ right.___

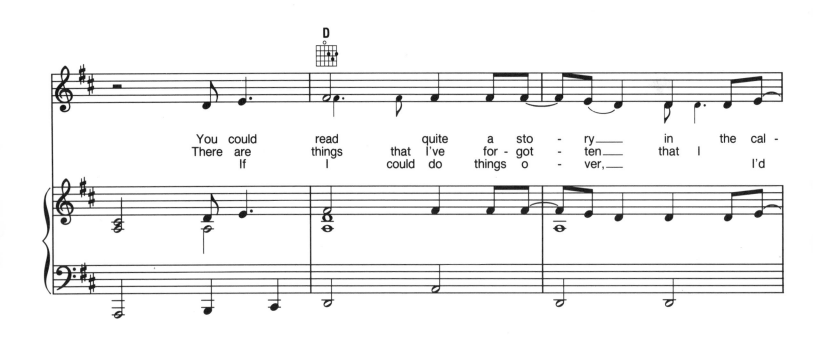

You could read quite a sto - ry___ in the cal -
There are things that I've for - got - ten___ that I
If I could do things o - ver,___ I'd

- lous - es___ and lines.___ Years of work___ and wor -
loved a - bout___ the man,___ but I'll al - ways re - mem -
live my life a - gain___ and nev - er take for grant -

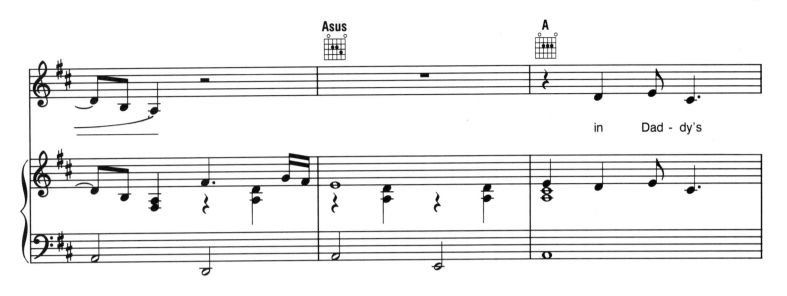

in Dad - dy's

hands.

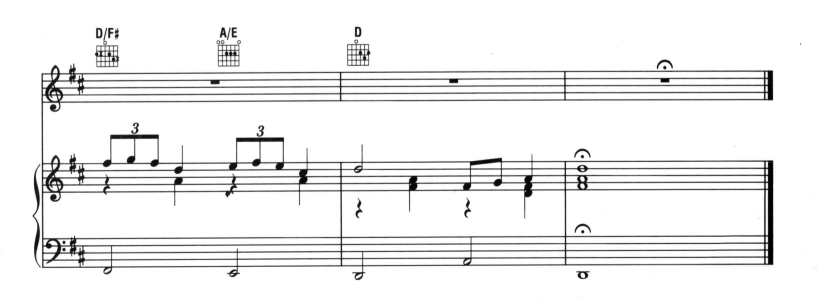

THE DANCE

Words and Music by
TONY ARATA

DO YA'

Words and Music by
K.T. OSLIN

DOES FORT WORTH EVER CROSS YOUR MIND

Medium Slow Country Swing

Words and Music by
SANGER D. SHAFER and DARLENE SHAFER

DON'T CLOSE YOUR EYES

Words and Music by BOB McDILL

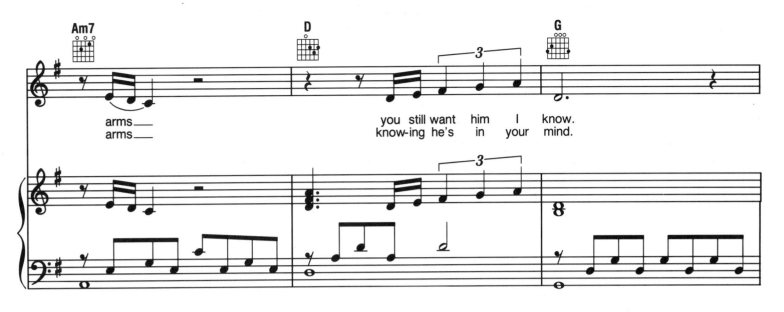

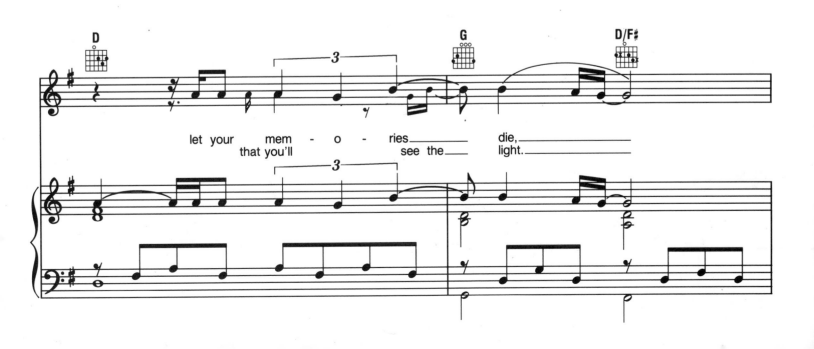

DON'T ROCK THE JUKEBOX

Words and Music by ALAN JACKSON
ROGER MURRAH and KEITH STEGALL

Additional Lyrics

2. I ain't got nothin' against rock and roll.
But when your heart's been broken, you need a song that's slow.
Ain't nothin' like a steel guitar to drown a memory.
Before you spend your money, babe, play a song for me.
Chorus

EIGHTEEN WHEELS AND A DOZEN ROSES

Words and Music by GENE NELSON
and PAUL NELSON

80'S LADIES

Moderately

Words and Music by
K.T. OSLIN

We were three — lit - tle girls — from school. —

One was pret - ty, one was smart, — and

one was a bor - der - line fool. —

Oh, she's still —

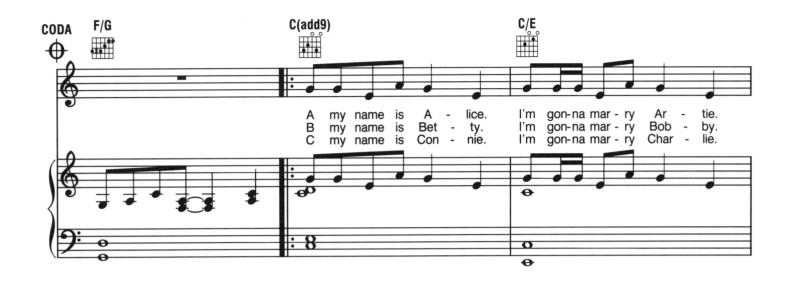

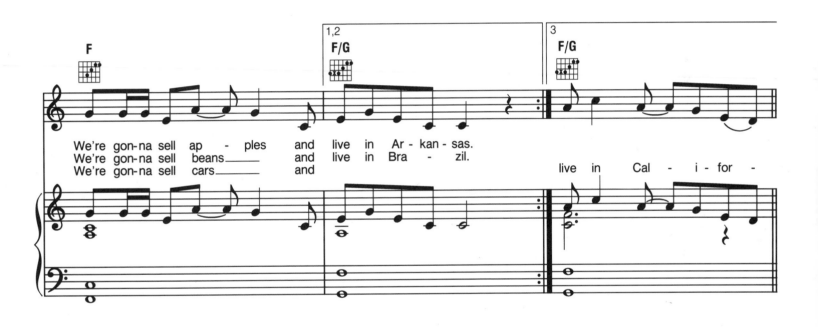

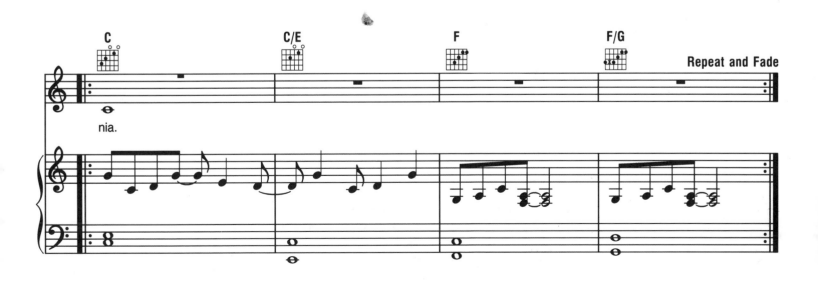

FRIENDS IN LOW PLACES

Words and Music by DEWAYNE BLACKWELL
and EARL BUD LEE

FOREVER AND EVER, AMEN

Words and Music by DON SCHLITZ
and PAUL OVERSTREET

MCA music publishing

GOD BLESS THE U.S.A.

Words and Music by
LEE GREENWOOD

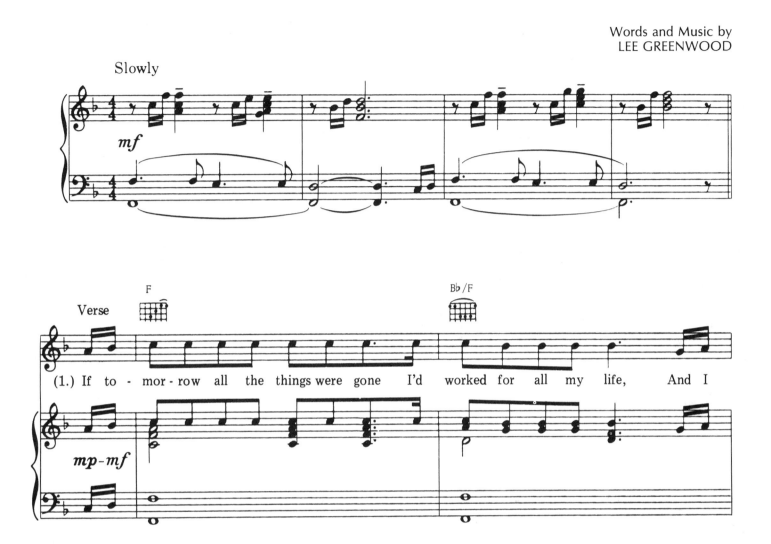

(1.) If to-mor-row all the things were gone I'd worked for all my life, And I

had to start a-gain ___ with just my chil-dren and my wife. I'd

GRANDPA
(TELL ME 'BOUT THE GOOD OLD DAYS)

Medium Slow Country

Words and Music by JAMIE O'HARA

107

HERE IN THE REAL WORLD

Words and Music by ALAN JACKSON
and MARK IRWIN

Cow - boys don't ___ cry, ___
See additional lyrics
and her - oes don't ___ die.

And good al - ways ___ wins ___ a - gain, ___ and a - gain. ___ And love is a

Additional Lyrics

2. I gave you my love, but that wasn't enough,
To hold your heart when times got tough.
And tonight on that silver screen, it'll end like it should,
Two lovers will make it through like I hoped we would.
Chorus

I TOLD YOU SO

Words and Music by
RANDY TRAVIS

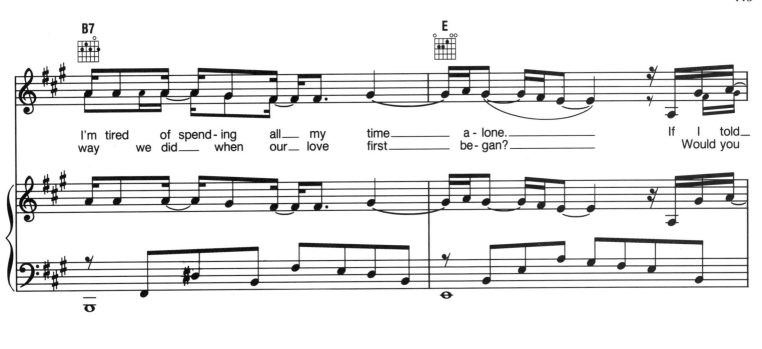

I'm tired of spend-ing all my time____ a - lone.____ If I told____
way we did____ when our love first____ be - gan?_____ Would you

____ you that I re - a - lize____ you're all____ I ev - er want - ed, and it's
tell me that you missed me too____ and that____ you've been so lone - ly, and you've

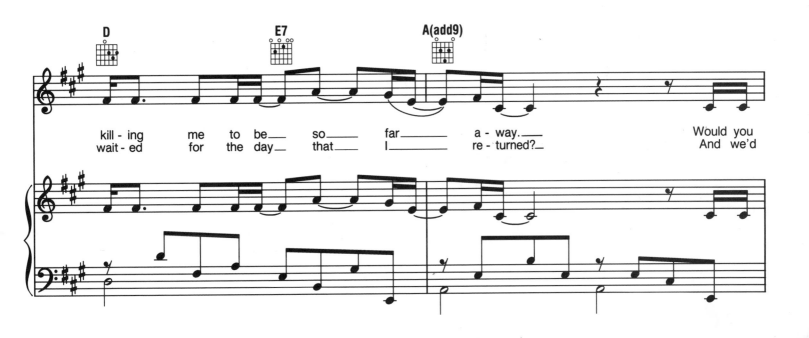

kill - ing me to be so____ far____ a - way.____ Would you
wait - ed for the day____ that____ I____ re - turned? And we'd

IF TOMORROW NEVER COMES

Words and Music by GARTH BROOKS
and KENT BLAZY

Additional Lyrics

2. 'Cause I've lost loved ones in my life.
Who never knew how much I loved them.
Now I live with the regret
That my true feelings for them never were revealed.
So I made a promise to myself
To say each day how much she means to me
And avoid that circumstance
Where there's no second chance to tell her how I feel. ('Cause)
Chorus

ISLANDS IN THE STREAM

Moderately Slow Rock

Words and Music by BARRY GIBB,
MAURICE GIBB and ROBIN GIBB

LIFE TURNED HER THAT WAY

Words and Music by
HARLAN HOWARD

KILLIN' TIME

Words and Music by CLINT BLACK
and HAYDEN NICHOLAS

A LITTLE GOOD NEWS

Words and Music by TOMMY ROCCO,
RORY BOURKE and CHARLIE BLACK

LOST IN THE FIFTIES TONIGHT
(IN THE STILL OF THE NIGHT)

Words and Music by MIKE REID,
TROY SEALS and FRED PARRISH

Additional Lyrics

These precious hours, we know can't survive.
Love's all that matters while the past is alive.
Now and for always, till time disappears,
We'll hold each other whenever we hear:

MAMA HE'S CRAZY

Words and Music by KENNY O' DELL

ON THE OTHER HAND

Words and Music by DON SCHLITZ
and PAUL OVERSTREET

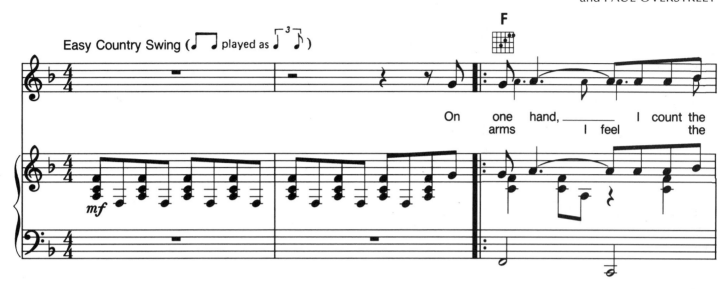

On one hand I could stay and be your lov-ing man,

but the rea - son I must go is on the oth-er hand.

In your Yeah, the

rea - son I must go is on the oth-er hand.

8va bassa

1982

Words and Music by BUDDY BLACKMON
and CARL VIPPERMAN

SEVEN SPANISH ANGELS

Words and Music by EDDIE SETSER
and TROY SEALS

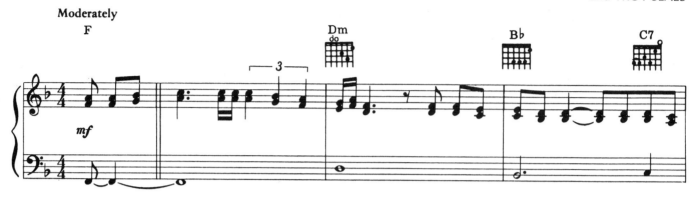

He looked down in-to__ her brown eyes and said, "Say a prayer__ for me." She
down and picked__ the gun up that lay smok-in' in__ his hand. She said,

threw her arms__ a-round him, whis-pered, "God will keep__ us free."__ They could
"Fa-ther, please__ for-give me, I can't make it with-out my man."__ And she

hear the ri - ders com - ing, he said, "This is my__ last fight. If they
knew the gun__ was emp - ty and she knew she could - n't win. But her

take me back__ to Tex - as _____ they won't take me back__ a - live."}
fi - nal prayer__ was an - swered__ when the ri - fles fired__ a - gain. }

There were

sev - en Span - ish an - gels at the al - tar of__ the sun._____

They were

TO ALL THE GIRLS I'VE LOVED BEFORE

Lyric by HAL DAVID
Music by ALBERT HAMMOND

Moderately slow, with expression

To all the girls I've loved be-fore,
once car-essed,
shared my life,

who trav-eled in and
and may I say I've
who now are some-one

out my door;
held the best;
els - e's wife;

I'm glad they came a - long,
for help-ing me to grow,
I'm glad they came a - long,

I ded - i - cate this
I owe a lot, I
I ded - i - cate this

WHEN I CALL YOUR NAME

Words and Music by TIM DUBOIS
and VINCE GILL

I rushed home from work, like I always
note on the table that told me good-

do. I spend my whole day just thinking of
bye, said you'd grown weary of living a

you. When I walked through the front door, my whole life was
lie. Oh, your love has ended, but mine still re-

THE WIND BENEATH MY WINGS

Words and Music by
LARRY HENLEY and JEFF SILBAR

Slowly flowing, in 2

It must have been cold___ there___ in my shad - ow,

to nev - er have sun - light on your face.

You've been con - tent___ to let me shine,

WHERE'VE YOU BEEN

Words and Music by DON HENRY
and JON VEZNER